Connect
with God's
Plan for
Your Future

Waiting

DOUG SAMPLES

Beacon Hill Press of Kansas City
Kansas City, Missouri

ISBN 083-411-8904

Printed in the
United States of America

Cover Design: Ted Ferguson
Cover Illustration: Keith Alexander

Library of Congress Cataloging-in-Publication Data

Samples, Doug, 1952-
Call waiting : connect with God's plan for your future / Doug Samples.
p. cm.
ISBN 0-8341-1890-4 (pbk.)
1. Vocation, Ecclesiastical. 2. Vocation—Christianity. I. Title.

BV4011.4 S36 2001
253'.2—dc21

2001018431

10 9 8 7 6 5 4 3 2

This book is dedicated
To my favorite rhino . . .
my dad:
Lawrence E. Samples

Everything
I have ever learned
I learned it first
from my dad!

Contents

Foreword

Doug Samples loves teens! He doesn't say it very often in this book, because he doesn't have to; it just comes out in every thought and on every page.

Because he loves you so deeply, Doug talks in a very straightforward manner. He uses terms you may not have heard in connection with youth, but by the time the conversation finishes, terms such as "cows," "rhinoceroses," "the Dumbo ride," "Highway 180," "the sweet aroma of orange blossoms," "the pilot light," and "smelly gas" make perfect sense.

I read this manuscript for the first time while on a recent trip to Africa. I was quite taken with the new thought of being a rhino rather than a cow. The very next morning we started on a one-day safari in the beautiful Masai Mara Reserve in Kenya. Believe it or not, we were fortunate enough to find one big, strong, massive, leadership-type rhino standing all alone under a tree in a most remote location in that vast land. It was just as Doug said, "As you go looking for rhinos, remember, you won't find them in herds." How did a college professor from Oklahoma know that?

God has also been speaking to me recently along another line: "Don't be a ho-hum Christian!" In my life it works out like this: Don't be a ho-hum disciple of Jesus, don't preach ho-hum sermons, don't read the Bible in a ho-hum manner, and don't project a ho-hum Christian image to others. Evidently God has been speaking to Doug Samples about the very same thing; he cries out against mediocrity—mediocre attitudes, thinking, jobs, churches, worship, grades, friendships. May the Holy Spirit remove the ho-hum—the mediocre—from the life of every one of us and fan the flame of God within our hearts into a powerful blaze.

I have a sense that this truth is not just for teens but for parents, grandparents, pastors, youth leaders, teachers, coaches, administrators, and even general superintendents as well. After reading *Call Waiting,* my first thought was that I must buy this book for Jayson, Derek, and Brooke, our three teenage grandchildren. After reading the book three times, I feel the same way—only more strongly. I deeply desire that my three teen grandchildren (and Dalton, Ashley, and Lexi, who are preteens) will grow up to be strong rhinos and not cows. My teen friend, that is also my prayer for you. Why settle for being a sparrow if God has made you to be an eagle?

Dr. Jim Diehl
General Superintendent, Church of the Nazarene

Introduction
Can We Talk?

Can we talk? I know I'm writing and you're reading, but can we just talk? I know it will be mostly a one-sided conversation ("What's that you said?"), but this book would be a lot more fun if we were sitting in a booth at Denny's having a Pepsi.

If we were face-to-face, I could watch your eyes light up when things clicked. When you started yawning, I would know to shut up. You would be able to tell me when my words do not make sense. But for now I guess I'll have to let these pages do the talking for me.

First, let me throw out a bunch of questions to get you thinking. What if you could do something really great with your life? What if you could invest your life in a way that would make a difference in your world? What if you could wake up every morning to a job that caused you to be challenged and excited about your day? What if you could fulfill your dreams and God's dream at the same time?

GET A LOAD OF THIS . . .
GOD WANTS YOU
FOR HIS TAG TEAM PARTNER!

Over the next few hours—or days—we spend talking together through the pages of this book, we will move far beyond the average questions that average teenagers are asking. We're going way past the routine hype of what's hot and what's not for this week or next. I am suggesting that you and I explore the mind-boggling possibility that God is inviting you to partner with Him in making a major impact on your world. I want to challenge you to think about how you are going to invest your life in ways that will result in your doing something great for God. After you realize what great plans God has waiting for your future, I am hoping you will use those dreams to shape who you are right now.

I originally planned to title this book *So You Think You're Called*. The thinking behind that title was that most young people get to *decide* what they are going to do with their lives. But then other young people are *called* by God to give their lives to the ministry. I planned to target this book to those *special* people who had been chosen by God to be called.

But while I was writing these pages, I decided I couldn't accept that thinking. I don't believe that God wants to call just a small group of teens to be full-time ministers while He lets all others pick their own favorite occupation.

I have become convinced that everyone is special in God's eyes, and therefore, He has a calling for everyone no matter what his or her lifework will be. That call can come in many shapes and sizes. It might come as a gradual dawning or a sudden thunderclap. God's call for your life might become clear to you over a period of years as you take inventory of the unique blend of talents, passions, and gifts He has built into your life. On the other hand, His call might come in a specific, unforgettable moment when He says, "This is it!"

When God says "This is it!" that call might make per-

> *His divine power has given us everything we need for life.*
> *2 Pet. 1:3*

fect sense or may take you totally by surprise. In other words, God's call may come as a confirmation of what you were wanting to do, or it may send you in a radically new direction.

My prayer is that whether you pastor a church or sell shoes at Payless, you will go after it with a call from God that generates a passion for greatness.

Our time together will be divided into two parts. We will start talking about how all of us, no matter what profession we feel called to, should plan to dream great dreams for God. We need to make sure our life counts for something great. If God has provided us everything we need for a life of greatness, we dare not settle for the mediocrity of average. The challenge of this first section is for all of us to live so that "whatever [we] do, whether in word or deed," it will all be done for the glory of God and "in the name of the Lord Jesus" (Col. 3:17).

In the second part, we will focus specifically on the idea of being called of God to full-time ministry as a pastor, youth pastor, missionary, and so on. Since I pastored over 20 years and now teach pastoral ministry to young college students, I have a special place in my heart for teenagers who feel their call is to the ministry. Although every call from God is special, a call to the ministry carries with it a unique significance.

Therefore, in the second part, if you are feeling called to the ministry, I hope to help you work through some of the issues you may be struggling with. We will be exploring such questions as these:

What does a call feel like?
How do I hear God's call?
How do I know if it is really from God?
What do I do if I have doubts?
What kinds of ministry are there to choose from?
How do I learn to be a good minister?

Even if you don't have a call to the ministry (or you're not clear where God is calling you), some of the material in the second part may prove beneficial as you sort out God's plan. Many of the same principles apply to those headed in other directions.

I'm excited to have this opportunity to talk with you about God's call and doing great things for Him. Hopefully, the time we spend together will be helpful as you make plans for your future. You might be one of the people God is calling to full-time Christian ministry. Then again, maybe not. The side of that fence you settle on is not really important. The critical matter is to prepare to live a life of greatness for God.

Before we go any farther, I need to ask that you promise to read about the pilot light in the last chapter. After reading all the other stuff, it is the last chapter that makes everything come together. If you skip that, you will have missed the whole reason for the book.

If you've made the promise, then we're ready to go.

Part 1

1

Everyone Is a Born Leader

Someone once asked the poet William Stafford, "When did you decide to be a poet?" Stafford responded, "Everyone was born a poet. I just kept doing it. The real question is, why did other people stop?"

That is exactly how I feel about leaders. I believe that everyone is a born leader. That means you too. No kidding. Every boy, every girl has been "fearfully and wonderfully made" (Ps. 139:14) and empowered by God to do great things. I'm sure you've found that verse in Jeremiah where God says He has great plans for you, "plans to prosper you and not to harm you, plans to give you hope and a future" (29:11).

Too often, however, we end up with only a few leaders and a lot of followers. In your group of friends at school or church, usually certain teenagers are considered leaders of the group, while others are seen as followers. You may be one of those leaders, or then again, you may fit in more among the followers. I am suggesting that everyone is a leader or at least can be if he or she wants to be.

Different Personalities for Different Leaders

Your world, your school, your church needs all kinds of leaders. How fascinating that God has created all kinds of people to fill all the places of leadership that are needed. A leader is not always just the person with one particular style of personality. That means that you, with all your unique talents, abilities, and gifts, have a place to serve as a leader. No matter what your personality style, the opportunities for leadership are wide open for you.

If you're like Scott and have the personality of a fun-loving, playful, creative, take-charge, show-offy, sometimes mischievous teenager, thousands of companies with leadership opportunities are waiting for you. At the other end of the spectrum are just as many companies looking for a leader like Mark, who is quieter, more introspective and reflective, who loves to do the detailed work of analytical thinking.

When you step out into the world, you will discover that every leadership position will have its own demands. New entrepreneurial companies will need a take-charge, risk-taking leader who's not afraid to try new things. At the same time, other companies will need a patient, calming influence to lead them through a time of corporate healing. An out-of-control business will need a detailed, analytical person at the helm, while a stagnant company with a bickering board of directors will look to an enthusiastic, fun-loving, people person to lead it back to health.

Different Personality Types

- Perfect Melancholics
- Peaceful Phlegmatics
- Popular Sanguines
- Powerful Cholerics

What's the point? I hope you will see that throughout your life there will always be a place—a business, family, church, and so on—that will need you to be at your best. God has a plan and a place for you. Whether it's now in your group at school and church, or whether it's 10 to 15 years from now in your profession, you need to be walking in tune with God on His journey toward greatness.

Throughout the Bible it is exciting to see how God calls different kinds of people for different tasks. Early in the Scriptures, God calls on the persistent, yet questioning skills of Moses "the melancholy" to lead His people out of Egypt. Later, two crazy fleeces convince the hesitant, uncertain, "leave me alone; I'm the weakest of the weak," Gideon "the phlegmatic" that he really is a mighty warrior. In the New Testament, Jesus is able to accomplish great purposes through both the strengths and weaknesses of Peter "the sanguine." And it is the strong-willed, take-charge Paul "the choleric" who pushes the young Christian Church out into the threatening Roman world.

With all these possibilities God unquestionably has leadership positions designed and waiting for you.

Different Levels for Different Leaders

While there are career positions that need various kinds of leaders, there are also an infinite number of leadership levels. The recognition that everyone is a born leader does not necessarily mean you are going to become the president of the United States. You may not even be the CEO of some huge Fortune 500 company.

But think for a minute about a man who becomes the night janitor for one of those Fortune 500 businesses. I am suggesting that even in this "lowly" position, far removed from what we usually call the real movers and shakers, the possibilities for leadership for this custodian are still endless:

- Excelling in his work each night prepares the way for those corporate heads who make global decisions throughout the day
- Listening with his patient attitude is an encouragement (and influence, i.e., act of leadership) to a fellow worker who is losing a spouse to cancer
- Coaching one of the local Little League baseball teams is admired by the nine-year-olds who think he is "pretty neat"
- Serving on the Buildings and Property Committee

at his church contributes a needed perspective, while his handyman skills are indispensable

- Providing for his family as a faithful husband and wrestling with his three sons in the living room after supper bring inner fulfillment

Even though this night janitor would not rank in anyone's list of Great American Leaders of Our Time, his leadership still has a significant ripple effect throughout his community. In my opinion, that makes him a great leader.

Whether you are planning to be the night janitor, the CEO of the company, or someone in between, you will always have a certain level of leadership influence to give to other people. The good news is—even if you are not the most popular kid at your school, even if you don't have a 4.0 GPA, even if you're not the student body president, even if you weren't voted most likely to succeed (but you did come in third as most likely to have a seed stuck between his teeth after lunch)—in God's eyes you still have tremendous leadership potential. He has creatively filled your life with just the right combination of natural talents, learned abilities, and spiritual gifts to make you exactly what He dreamed you to be. He has unbelievably great plans laid out for you. Are you ready to join Him on the journey?

Just in Case

Just in case you still don't believe me when I say that everyone is a born leader, just in case you are still thinking that this leadership/greatness stuff is for someone other than you, just in case you're still saying, "I'm not bright enough" or "I've got too many strikes against me," let me leave you with this final thought: "A study of three hundred highly successful people, people like Franklin Delano Roosevelt, Helen Keller, Winston Churchill, Albert Schweitzer, Mahatma Gandhi, and Albert Einstein, reveals that one-fourth had handicaps, such as blindness, deafness, or crippled limbs. Three-fourths had either been born in poverty, came from broken homes, or at least came from exceedingly tense or disturbed situations" (John Maxwell, *Developing the Leader Within You,* 80).

2

But What If I Get Sick on Dumbo?

"OK, so God has a great plan for my life. But how am I supposed to find out what that plan is? What if I decide to be a great engineer, but He wanted me to be a great electrician? I sure don't want to mess things up. How do I know for sure that I am going in the direction He wants me to go? Why is it so hard to figure this out?"

Don't ever forget how much God loves you!

Before you have a panic attack and think you have missed God's will before your 18th birthday, let's back up and remember just how much God loves you. Let's remember how much He wants to help you discover His design for you.

I am convinced that God loves you too much to let you just "mess things up." And I'm convinced that if you will keep your heart tender to God's daily direction, you will learn to discern His will and His call for your life.

During your growing-up years . . .

- You will watch certain talents and abilities develop.
- You will discover interests that you are really passionate about.
- You will learn that your personality is unique.

- You will notice that you work better with your hands than with your head (or vice versa).
- You will realize that some things come very natural to you, while others are extremely awkward.

All these factors are part of the blueprint God built into you. It is not an accident that you have the specific collection of qualities that you do. It's not as though God put you together and then said, "Wow! What am I gonna do with this mess?" He knew exactly what He was doing. He deliberately built you for a purpose. He lovingly and tenderly brought together an infinite number of incredible ingredients to create the person called "You."

I like to think that God has a full set of blueprints for us in His head. In Ps. 139:13-15 it says, "For you created my inmost being; you knit me together in my mother's womb. I praise you because I am fearfully and wonderfully made . . . My frame was not hidden from you when I was made in the secret place."

When I read where David wrote about "my frame," I imagine him saying to God, "You knew my blueprint from the very beginning of my life. From day one, You knew my DNA without even putting it under a microscope. You are the One who first wrote this computer program called 'My Life' that I am now experiencing."

From the very moment you are conceived, God already sees the infinite possibilities of your life. As you live your life, you get to explore those possibilities on a day-to-day basis without knowing for sure what direction your journey is headed.

In the early years, you are sometimes overwhelmed by the challenge of trying to figure out exactly what it is you are supposed to be doing with your life. You question God and yourself: "What am I supposed to do in life? What does God want me to be?"

"But I Have to Find His Will!"

Can I offer a suggestion? I wonder sometimes if we

stress out way too much about this. I wonder if we bang on heaven's door begging God to show us what His will is for our lives when He wants to say, "Hey, guys, you are making this a lot harder than it should be. This is not some complex mystery that you have to solve and 'get right' in order to find My will for your life. Relax."

Maybe finding God's will is not so much hearing some booming voice from heaven that tells us what to do with the rest of our lives. Maybe it's more like asking God to help us see clearly the blueprint He has already built into us.

I heard about a guy in Dallas who was walking down the street one day and looked down to see the letters "GPC" painted on the sidewalk. He immediately took it to be a sign from God to "Go Preach Christ!" The only problem was, he was a terrible preacher. Many of his church members wondered if the letters on the sidewalk had really meant "Go Plant Corn!"

God's call will usually fit hand-in-hand with the talents, abilities, personality, and passion He has already built into our lives. For instance:

- If you are 6'2" and weigh 205, God is probably not going to call you to be a jockey!
- If you have the eyesight of a mole, God is probably not going to call you to be a fighter pilot.
- If you get sick on the Dumbo ride at Disneyland, God is probably not going to call you to be an astronaut.
- If you have trouble grasping the concept of multiplication, God is probably not going to call you to be a stockbroker on Wall Street.

Yes, I will admit there are notable exceptions (Beethoven wrote his Ninth Symphony when he was totally deaf). Yes, it is true God can call untalented people to do outstanding accomplishments. (Check out Gideon in chapter 6.) And, yes, if God places a definite but unusual call on your life, you should follow that call and trust that He knows what He's doing.

However, you might be more successful in your search for God's will if you incorporate some new questions into your prayers. Instead of the same old "What do You want me to do with my life?" how about some new ones like these:

- What have You made me good at?
  The piano?
  Math skills?
  Public speaking?
- What is it You have made me really passionate about?
  Medicine and healing?
  Creating new businesses?
  Remodeling old cars?
- Have You designed me with more head skills or hand skills?
  Physics or plumbing?
  Advertising or athletics?
  Judge or janitor?

Once you begin to collect some data in your conversations with God about these matters, you may well be on your way to discovering the *you* God has been dreaming about all along.

Please don't misunderstand me. I am not suggesting you make a list of your strengths and weaknesses and then just decide what you want to do with your life. To search for your life's calling without the help of God's leadership is asking for lots of dead-end streets. Throughout the Book of Judges, when "everyone did what was right in his own eyes" (21:25), ignoring divine direction, the result was not pretty.

But one part of discovering God's will is evaluating yourself in the light of God's blueprint and asking God to help you see the person He has built into you. As a part of this growing, discerning process you will want to ask God to confirm what you are seeing with His own calling. Keep telling God what you are learning about yourself, and then ask if your spiritual eyesight is accurate. Let Him know that if at any time you misinterpret some factor, He has total freedom to hit the Refresh button and make it clear what the signal meant. Remind Him (and yourself) that He always has the right to "drop a new rock in the pond" that creates new ripples for you (and Him) to sort out.

When I am faced with a critical decision and God has not made His will clearly known to me, I often find myself praying a prayer like this: "God, based on everything I know, it seems the best thing for me to do in this situation is ABC. Now, if You want me to do something different (like XYZ), then You need to let me know. So, unless I hear from You, I'm going to keep going down the ABC path and assume that is Your will for this situation. But remember, I want Your will more than anything, so all You need to do if I've missed Your signal is to let me know!"

ABC or XYZ?

Here's the deal: you want to know God's will for your life, and He wants you to know His will. He has already built some clues regarding that plan into the design fabric of your life. If you are observant, you will be able to see some of that. And if you are listening, you will hear the confirmation of His call.

And if by chance you misread the signals and head off in the wrong direction, He will let you know. All you need to do is stay tender.

3

Doing Something Great for God

To be honest, I'm not overly concerned about you missing God's will for your life. I have lots of confidence in your desire to be obedient and even more confidence in God's ability to reveal His plan to you.

In the whole scheme of God's overall plan, it doesn't really matter whether you are a waitress, a junior high science teacher, a pastor, or a stay-at-home mom. His big plan is simply to get His people out into His world in order to be His witnesses.

Whatever it is we are doing in life, the important thing is to be able to answer yes to three basic questions:

1. Do you have a calling?
2. Are you going to live with passion?
3. Are you going to do something great for God with your life?

Do You Have a Calling?

From our discussion in the last chapter, the point worth reemphasizing is this: Whatever career you pursue as your life mission, you need to know that God has called you to that profession. If you're going to get up every morning at 6 A.M. to go to work, you need to know that God has called you to that profession.

It is hard to stay motivated day in and day out if you do not have a purpose and mission in life. That's why it is so important during your early years to find God's design and plan for your life. When you know that you are doing what God designed you for, there is a great feeling of fulfillment that makes life more enjoyable.

God desperately needs people who feel called to the profession of nursing. He needs people who are called to be journalists. He needs good, strong Christian people in the office complex, the oil field, the factory, the post office, and the symphony.

God might call you to be an emergency room trauma specialist for a whole bunch of reasons: (1) He knows you would be good at it. (2) He knows you would make lots of families happy by saving their loved ones from the brink of death. (3) He knows you would be a great witness to your fellow doctors and nurses. (4) He knows your tithe money would help build a new gymnasium at the church you attend. (5) He knows you are humble enough to do all this awesome stuff and not get a big head.

So don't just decide what you want to do in life. Ask God to reveal to you His unique blueprint so you can hear His calling whatever it might involve. With God's direction, you will not have just a job or even a career; you will have a life mission.

Are You Going to Live Life with Passion?

Let me try to say it again with a new twist; I'm not concerned about whether you are a podiatrist or a pastor. What I am very concerned about is whether you are going to live your life with fire and passion and greatness.

"Timothy, it's your turn to fan the flame!"

In 2 Tim. 1:6 Paul has these words for Timothy: "Fan into flame the gift of God, which is in you." Sounds innocent enough until you understand that these are some of Paul's last words. He is in prison. He's about to die.

He is calling out to Timothy, "My time is almost up. I've run my race. Timothy, it's your turn. It's up to you now. You need to burn with the fire and passion of God in your life. God has put His gift of greatness into you, and you need to fan that fire into a roaring blaze!"

But when we try to translate that 1st-century cry into the 21st century, we are faced with a huge problem. Today's American culture is not into passion and fire and roaring blazes. America today is into mediocrity. We like to be average. We prefer the middle of the pack. Lukewarm feels pretty nice to us—not too hot and not too cold.

Did you know that not long ago the number one T-shirt in Japan was "We're No. 1!" That same year in the United States, the number one T-shirt was "Underachiever and Proud of It!"

Oh, how I wish I could convince you to hate mediocrity. How I wish you would hate

mediocre food	mediocre jobs
mediocre plans	mediocre attitudes
mediocre churches	mediocre children
mediocre thinking	mediocre life
mediocre worship	mediocre future
mediocre books	mediocre classes
mediocre grades	mediocre friendships

Don't accept mediocrity. Don't be satisfied with average. Get rid of all that's mediocre in your life and replace it with passion. Get excited about life. Get excited about school. Get excited about your family. Get excited about your youth group. Get excited about being a global Christian. Get excited about the future. Get excited about *Jesus!*

Are You Going to Do Something Great for God?

One more time. . . . I know you are anxious to know what profession or career God has for your life, but the bigger question is this: Whatever you do in life, are you going to do something great for God?

I am hearing a growing number of young people who are saying, "I'm going to have a job, but what I'm really excited about is doing ministry in the church for Jesus." "I plan to be an airline pilot, but my real love is serving Jesus." "I'm looking forward to being a teacher, but that will just be my job. What really has me pumped is being involved in the compassionate ministry of my church down at the homeless center."

This idea of doing great things for God obviously means getting radically involved in the life and mission of your local church. However, it can also stretch way beyond the walls of your church. I want to challenge you to find ways within your chosen profession to accomplish things that bring glory and praise to God.

- If you're going to be a carpenter, then build great houses.
- If you're going to repair cars, give your customers the best service of anybody in the city.
- If you're going to be a stay-at-home mom, then raise some great kids.
- If you're going to be a musician, create a new sound that appeals to multigenerations.
- If you're going to be a computer whiz, design some cool video games that teach values instead of violence to our children.

Howard Hendricks tells the story of an unforgettable flight attendant he met one day. The airplane was crowd-

Service with a Smile!

ed with people, and it seemed as if everybody was crabby and fussy. There were several babies on the flight taking turns filling the air with their crying and whining. Adding to the turmoil was sporadic air turbulence that made it difficult for the flight attendants to serve the meal.

But there was one flight attendant who never let the restlessness of the flight get to her. Even at 30,000 feet she seemed to operate on a higher level than everyone else. When she caught the rude end of someone's temper, she always responded with kindness. When people complained about the bumpy flight, she did her best to calm them down. She even found some new toys to help entertain the fussy babies. And to top it off, she handled all these hassles with a bright, cheerful smile.

As the flight was coming to a close, Howard had a chance to speak to the flight attendant. He said, "Delta Airlines is awfully lucky to have someone like you working for them!" She surprised Howard by responding, "I don't work for Delta." Howard asked, "Are you part of some independent flight attendant union?" "No," she replied with a soft smile. "Well, then, who *do* you work for?" Howard wondered. With an even bigger grin she announced, "I work for Jesus. Delta just signs my checks."

Please don't go through life working a boring nine-to-five job and then sitting in your easy chair all night flipping channels.

- During these early years of your life, listen to God as He helps you discern the life mission He has designed for you.
- Begin now to replace all the mediocrity in your life with passion.
- Decide right now that "no matter who signs my paycheck, I'm always working for Jesus."

4
Don't Be a Cow . . . Be a Rhinoceros

Has anyone ever taken the time to explain to you the difference between a cow and a rhinoceros? It's all about attitude. Some people have cow attitudes, while others have rhino attitudes.

Cows

- Cows love to lie around all day, chew their cud, and moo, which is their way of complaining.
- Cows love to be lazy and hang out all day with nothing to do.
- Cows are always looking for shortcuts and the path of least resistance.
- Cows love to wait around and watch to see which way the herd is going.
- Cows are always content with a C on a test, especially when it would mean another two or three hours of study to get a B or an A.
- Most of all, cows love mediocrity. They dream of being ordinary and average.

Rhinoceroses

On the other hand . . .

- Rhinos are thick-skinned chargers who enjoy the excitement of running through the jungle of life rather than following the herd of cows to the meat market.
- Rhinos love a great challenge.

- Rhinos love the risks, the demands, and even the potential failures that come with the hazards of life.
- Rhinos love swimming upstream.
- Rhinos love being five minutes early for a 6 A.M. basketball practice.
- Rhinos love to have the ball in their hands in the final seconds with the game on the line.
- Rhinos love being the lead dogs with bugs in their teeth.
- Rhinos are great dreamers.
- Rhinos are never afraid of failure because every time they fail they get smarter.
- Rhinos understand that "success is going from failure to failure without losing enthusiasm." (That's an Abraham Lincoln quote.)

Here's the bottom line: Being a rhinoceros is looking to see which way everybody else is going and then going in the opposite direction.

Rhinos in the Jungles of West Virginia

My dad taught me at an early age to be a rhinoceros. While all the other dads were joining country clubs and playing golf with their sons, my dad bought a nasty piece of wooded hillside called Knollwood. There must have been a gazillion trees on this three acres of West Virginia hillside. Our job was to clear out over half the trees in

Cows take a poll to find the way.
Rhinos lead the way.

Cows say, "The world owes me a living."
Rhinos say, "I owe the world my best."

Cows have problems.
Rhinos have opportunities.

Cows are satisfied with the status quo.
Rhinos are always looking for the new thing God is wanting to do.

Cows want to lie around.
Rhinos want to change the world.

order to make room for a house, a driveway, and so on. During my junior high and senior high years, Dad and I would get up early on Saturday mornings and throughout the summer to grub out trees. Dad didn't believe in cutting the tree off at the ground and leaving the stump. Nooooooooo! Every tree had to be dug out (grubbed out) by the roots and then cut up with a two-man saw or an ax. (Chain saws must have been against Dad's religion.)

Every morning as Dad and I would drive to Knollwood, I would cry and complain and fuss in hopes that Dad would somehow be struck with a miracle of mercy and let me go back home and sleep in. I wanted to be a cow like all my other cow friends and sleep till 11 A.M. and then go play baseball or basketball and go down to the riverbank and tell dirty stories.

But my dad never allowed me to be a cow. He taught me to work hard while everyone else was playing. He taught me to grub out a tree while everyone else was leaving the stump. He taught me to think while everyone else was goofing off. He taught me to solve problems while everyone else was standing around complaining. He taught me to dream the impossible while everyone else was saying it couldn't be done. He taught me to commit my life to God while all my friends were being cows down on the riverbank.

Back then I really hated those days of working and sweating down at Knollwood. But now I wouldn't trade them for the world. Those were the days I was a junior rhino in training.

Are You a Rhino?

Here's what is most exciting for me: just the fact that you are reading this book means you already qualify as a potential rhinoceros. (If someone bought it for you, then he or she must think you've got some rhino in you.) Just the fact that you are holding this book in your tiny little rhino paws (hooves?) tells me that there is something down inside of you that doesn't want to accept just being average. If you are still reading this far into the book, then it's for sure you are one of those people who dream of doing great things for God.

But I've got to warn you: If you choose to be a rhinoceros, you will always be the target of a lot of criticism and hassle from all the other cows. They will continually try to pull you back into the herd so that you'll be average and plain and common and mediocre like the rest of them.

"Where do you think you're going?"

"Who do you think you are?"

"Who are you trying to impress?"

"Someone ought to take you down a notch or two!"

"Why did you have to mess up the curve for that test?"

"Why don't you want to hang out with us anymore? Aren't we good enough for you?"

Let's Kill the Rhino

One of the great rhinos of the Bible faced this same kind of harassment early in his life. In Gen. 37 Joseph is beginning to flex his rhino muscles, telling his father and brothers about these rhino dreams he has been having. In the dreams, God is giving Joseph a sneak preview of some of the unbelievably great things that are going to happen in his life. His cow brothers are not too thrilled to see their little brother talking as if he's the big rhino king of the jungle. So, one day when Joseph is coming to see them out in the fields, they say to themselves, "Here comes that dreamer [rhino]! . . . let's kill him" (vv. 19-20). (Check out the rest of the story to see how this rhino not only survives their attack but also comes charging back to save the day.)

Here's the key: when all the cows are disapproving of what you are doing, then you know you're doing the right stuff. Maybe this is what the Bible is trying to tell us when it says, "Wide is the gate and broad is the road that leads to destruction, and many enter through it. But small is the gate and narrow the road that leads to life, and only a few [rhinos] find it" (Matt. 7:13-14, with one extra word included for emphasis).

Don't be a cow and follow the crowd. Hook up your horn to Jesus, and follow Him no matter what anyone else is saying or doing.

Look for Other Rhinos

Instead of hanging around with all the cows, you need to find some other rhino friends to team up with. As you go looking for rhinos, remember, you won't find them in herds. They will undoubtedly be unique people who may not be on the most popular list. There may even be some great rhinos hiding in the senior adult group at your church from whom you could learn some valuable lessons, if you would carve out some time to be with them.

GREAT RHINOS IN HISTORY

Maybe it would help if I showed you some of the great rhinos in history so you would know what they look like. Thomas Edison was a rhino who failed a thousand times trying to invent a lightbulb, but he never gave up. Orville and Wilbur Wright built a flying machine while all the other cows were standing around saying it couldn't be done. John Glenn went up into space as an astronaut for a second time when he was 77 years old. Beethoven composed some of his greatest works late in his life after he had become totally deaf. Martin Luther nailed his Ninety-five Theses on the church door at Wittenberg, which got him in trouble but initiated the great Reformation in the Church. Martin Luther King Jr.

had a dream at a time when everyone else was consumed by a nightmare. Bill Gates was dreaming of a personal computer in every home in America just a few years after the chairman of IBM had declared, "I think there is a world market for maybe five computers." Don Quixote, my rhino hero, could look at an Aldonza and see a Dulcinea. Three Hebrew teenagers (Shadrach, Meshach, and Abednego) each politely but boldly told the king, "I'm no cow, so I won't bow!"

Why Be a Rhino?

By this time some of you are probably into this whole rhino thing. But some of you may still be asking the question why. "Why do I have to be a rhino? Why can't I be a cow and just take life easy? Being a rhino sounds like a lot of hard work."

Here's the reason. Are you ready? The reason you need to be a rhino instead of a cow is because the world out there is a *jungle* and not a *pasture field*. It really is a jungle out there. And if a cow gets loose in the jungle, it's not going to be the king of the jungle; it's going to be the Burger King of the jungle. The world is not an easy place. It's not fair. It's not safe.

The world out there is challenging, demanding, risky, dangerous, and hazardous. You will never survive, you will never make it, if you're a cow. But when you decide to be a rhino, you are choosing to enjoy the adventures and opportunities of life. You are choosing to take life by storm even when it means fighting through failures and disappointments.

As a rhino you will discover that the Bible is the most amazing safari guide Manual anyone has ever written. Throughout the pages of God's Word you and I can find the kind of spiritual food that keeps a rhino going strong. Stuff like

- "In all your ways acknowledge [God], and He shall direct your paths" (Prov. 3:6, NKJV).

- "I can do all things through Christ who strengthens me" (Phil. 4:13, NKJV).
- "Consider it pure joy, my brothers, whenever you face trials of many kinds, because you know that the testing of your faith develops perseverance. Perseverance must finish its work so that you may be mature and complete, not lacking anything" (James 1:2-3).
- "We are hard pressed on every side, but not crushed; perplexed, but not in despair; persecuted, but not abandoned; struck down, but not destroyed" (2 Cor. 4:8).
- "Therefore we do not lose heart. Though outwardly we are wasting away, yet inwardly we are being renewed. . . . For our light and momentary troubles [only a rhino could see dying as a light and momentary trouble] are achieving for us an eternal glory that far outweighs them all" (2 Cor. 4:16-17).

Choose or Moos?

Well, it's time for Final Jeopardy. Before we go any further in this book, we need to settle this rhino thing once and for all. Go get a pen, and check the box that applies:

☐ **Yes, I choose greatness!**

☐ **No, thank you. I want to be mediocre.**

Fantastic! Now let's get on with it.

> If you would like to read more about being a rhino, I would encourage you to contact Scott Alexander at Rhino Press, P.O. Box 2303520, Laguna Hills, CA 92564. He has written three books about "Rhinocerology" that have been foundational to my adoption of the rhino as one of my favorite heroes.

THE RHINO CREED

- **People are unreasonable, illogical, and self-centered . . . love them anyway!**
- **If you do good, people will accuse you of selfish motives . . . do good anyway!**
- **If you are successful, you will have false friends and true enemies . . . succeed anyway!**
- **The good you do today will be forgotten tomorrow . . . do good anyway!**
- **Honesty and truthfulness make you vulnerable . . . be honest and truthful anyway!**
- **The biggest people with the biggest ideas can be shot down by the smallest people with the smallest minds . . . think big anyway!**
- **What you spend years building may be destroyed overnight . . . build anyway!**
- **Give the world the best you've got, and you'll get kicked in the teeth . . . give the world the best you've got anyway!**

Part 2

5
What About a Call to Full-time Ministry?

How's your Pepsi holding out? Need a refill? "Waiter, another round of drinks please and an order of fries to munch on."

I hope it's starting to sink in that God has a great life ahead of you. Embedded in your blueprint design are rich talents, abilities, passions, personality strengths, and spiritual gifts that are yours to discover and develop. If you keep your heart tender to God's calling and cultivate a huge rhino attitude, you are going to do great things for God no matter what your lifework is.

As we move into this new section, I want to turn a corner in our discussion and ask some new questions. We mentioned in chapter 3 that God always has the right to "drop a new rock in the pond" that creates new ripples in your life. Here's my first new question: What if you're going along minding your own business, getting good grades, behaving yourself (most of the time), growing with God, and trying to figure out what kind of job you need to help you buy the latest new hot car—and then, all of a sudden, God drops this new rock in your pond: "Hey, I want you to be a pastor." What would you do? How would you respond? Would you say yes, or would you try to find a nice way to tell God, "You're crazy"?

Maybe you don't think that could ever happen to you. My friend Chad didn't either. Here is his story about how

God surprised him. **"I was at the altar praying with one of my friends when I realized I needed to pray for myself. I slid over, found my own spot, and started to pray. Then, although it wasn't an audible voice, I heard God speaking to my innermost being, and He said, 'Missions.' I said, 'You've got to be kidding!' At first I didn't even want to think about a call to missions, but every year since then my call has gotten stronger. Now it's almost all I ever think about."**

You've got to be kidding!

God obviously does not want to call every teenager into full-time ministry, but I do think He would love for every teenager to be open to a call to ministry.*

As you grow in your relationship with the Lord, there ought to be times when you check your signals with Him. I can see you having a conversation with God where you say, "God, I'm doing my best to follow Your direction. As of right now it seems as if You're leading me into marine biology. And I'm excited about that. But I just want to remind You that if You want to interrupt those plans and call me to give the first 10 years of my life teaching on the mission field, I'll be glad to readjust. 'Cause all I really want to do is follow Your will for my life."

If you were to pray that prayer, you might hear God respond, "No, you're doing great! I like where we're headed. But thanks for asking."

---

*In the first section of the book we said that everyone, no matter what his or her profession, should be involved in ministry doing great things for God. Here in the second half, when we use the term *ministry,* we are referring to the full-time profession of a minister (i.e., pastor, youth pastor, missionary, etc.).

Some of you, however, might feel as if God is calling you to the ministry. For some, that call has already come through loud and clear and you are pursuing it. For others, you are still praying hard trying to figure out for sure if you are really called. There is no simple one-two-three formula I can give you to help you know for sure if you are specifically called to the ministry. No one can tell you that for certain. That is something you ultimately have to work out between you and God.

For the rest of our time together, I'd like to come alongside you on your journey so we can talk about what it's like to have a call to the ministry. Maybe we can raise some issues and answer some questions that will help you in your desire to know God's will for your life.

Advice from the Experts

I remember what it was like when God called me into the ministry. I remember how excited I was, and I'd love to tell you about it sometime. But for now I want to do something even better. I have a bunch of college friends who have felt a definite call to the ministry and are now studying for it. I asked them a series of questions that they responded to. Those responses have given me insights to help me write this book. I am sharing their responses to two main questions you might be struggling with. As you listen to their stories, you will learn more about your own call.

How Did Your Call First Come?

A call from God is like a snowflake: no two are exactly alike. God never runs out of unique ways to get His message to us. There is no "one perfect way" for a call to come. Here you will read some of the ways teenagers have heard God's call. You might find a story that sounds similar to yours. Then again, yours may be 100 percent unique.

"All my life I knew that God wanted me for something big. When He saw how passionate I was about leading praise and worship at my church, He began to show me that I should pursue that as my lifework." —Nathan

"When I was a little boy, there were two things I wanted to do: build skyscrapers and be a pastor. By the time I reached fifth grade I wanted to be the first chaplain in a space station. During my junior high years God made it clear I was to be a pastor. It was something I could never get away from." —Ben

"When I was 15, I was at church camp. I had really been struggling to know what I was supposed to do with my life. My youth pastor had been praying with me about it. Then one night that week it just came to me: 'I want you to be a youth pastor.' What a relief to finally know!" —Brandon

"I first began to feel my call when I was riding around with a basketball friend who had a call to the ministry. We got to talking about our future and what we were going to do with our lives. That's when God started talking to me. Over the next couple of years it grew stronger. When our youth group was on a mission trip to Fort Worth, Texas, God let me know for sure that He was calling me to work with inner-city youth." —Chad

"My mother tells me that when I was three and four I would set up my stuffed animals and preach to them. But it was not until my senior year of high school that God confirmed that call. One night when I was visiting my regional college, God suddenly and definitely called me into the ministry." —Chris

"I received my call the summer before my senior year of high school. I was ready for God to do more new stuff in my life. While I was at church camp, God confirmed to me what His plans were. Looking back now, I can pick out instances where God may have been telling me the exact same thing, but it was that night at camp that I accepted God's call for my life."

—Jeremy

"My call has been with me for so long that I can't remember ever not having it. It's as if this was what I was created to do." —Mary

"I can remember when all the other kids wanted to be firemen, I wanted to be a preacher. But I don't think I really 'felt a call' until my early teen years when the people of my church informed me that I was going 'to be a preacher someday.'" —Michael

"You're not going to believe this, but it's true. I was watching cartoons on Saturday morning when I was 10. During a commercial, I was flipping channels and found this low-budget Christian TV channel. They had a cheesy skit about people smuggling Bibles into Russia. It was full of bad humor, poor acting, and corny lines. But that's the occasion God used to call me to the ministry." —Rodger

"It just happened one day when I saw that it was possible to give my whole life to something that I thoroughly enjoyed and that brought me extreme fulfillment. That something was working with children."

—Sara

"It came very quietly and softly at a youth gathering at my regional college. God used the speaker to let me know that He wanted me as a teacher on the mission field."

—Stephanie

"When I was 10 I was reading a children's missionary book and when the girl in the story told God

she would be obedient and go, I felt a really strange feeling. I was wondering what had happened. I said, 'God, if that was You, please do it again.' He did. So, now I'm studying for the mission field." —Meagan

How Did Your Call Feel?

We always hear people say, "I felt God's call." I asked my friends to describe what that "feeling" felt like. Here's what they said. (I'd love to know what your call felt like.)

"It felt as if God was tugging at my heart." —Zach

"When I first became aware of my call I was so excited . . . It was like my first kiss!" —Tyler

"My call felt like a quiet whisper at first, but now it has become a war cry in my heart." —B. J.

"My call came as a surprise. It was kind of scary at first. I didn't think God could use me, so it came as a shock to me." —Justin

"My call makes me feel like if I were to do anything else other than full-time ministry, I would be wasting my time." —Joshua

"My call came like a yearning to help other people and also like a desire to do more with my life." —Paige

"To me my call felt like an illumination. It's like when you hold a tube up to your eye and you're looking through it. You can only see what is right in front of you. God's call was like taking the tube away. Suddenly I could see things I had no idea were there. Things just began to make sense and fall into place." —Chad

"My call feels like my shadow. It is always there

like an ever-present burning within my heart. My call always reminds me of my purpose in life."
—Stephanie

"It was like a realization of something I should have known all along but I never knew it. Like, 'Oh, duh! Be a youth pastor!'" —Andrew

"Anytime I would think about being a pastor there would be this persistent urging that I never could get away from. After a while I realized this was God's way of calling me to the ministry." —Brad

"It wasn't as if God used audible words to speak to me. It was like a pressing on my heart—as if God took a hot branding iron and pressed it against my heart. One minute it wasn't there, and the next minute it was. That's when God showed me He wanted me to be a missionary. For four years I tried to run from God's call. Finally one night all my strength was gone. It drained out of me like water draining from a broken pot. Self spilled out on the ground until I was empty. Then God filled me with himself. As I wept and prayed, I surrendered completely to God. I told God I would do anything He wanted me to do. But I did have one request. I clearly remember my prayer: 'Lord, I'll do anything that You ask of me. If You want me to go into the ministry, I will. If You want me to be a missionary, I will. Whatever You want is Yours. I'll do anything You want, but I would do it much better if You would give me the desire to do it. Please, Lord, change my desire so that this is what I want to do. Then I can do it with all my heart. Still, even

GOD TOOK A HOT BRANDING IRON TO MY HEART

if You don't give me that desire, I will do it anyway because I desire to serve You!' Before I even opened my eyes, God lit a fire in my heart that still burns strong today."

—Rodger

Can God Really Use Me?

Some of you who think you have a call to ministry may be struggling with another kind of question. There may be stuff in your past that you are not proud of. You may have messed up your life so bad that you're not sure if God can actually use someone like you.

Well, the good news is God forgives! When we confess the sins of our past and tell Him how sorry we are, then He wipes our screen completely clean. He gives us a second chance. If you are wondering if God can use a person like you in His ministry, remember, you're in good company because

Moses stuttered.
David's armor didn't fit.
John Mark was rejected by Paul.
Timothy had ulcers.
Hosea's wife was a prostitute.
Amos was a grade school dropout.
Jacob was a liar.
David had an affair.
Solomon was too rich.
Abraham was too old.
David was too young.
Peter was afraid of death.
Lazarus was dead.
John was self-righteous.
Naomi was a widow.
Paul was a murderer.
Moses was too.
Jonah ran from God.
Miriam was a gossip.
Gideon and Thomas both doubted.

Jeremiah was depressed and suicidal.
Elijah was burned out.
John the Baptist was a loudmouth.
Martha was a worrywart.
Mary was lazy.
Samson had long hair.
Noah got drunk.
Peter, Paul, and Moses all had short tempers.

If God can use all of those people, I'm sure He can find a place for you and me.

One More Story

Before we leave this chapter on discerning God's call to the ministry, I have a story from my friend Ryan for you. I think you'll like it.

"Hesitantly, I pull the lid off the box. Closing my fingers around the bottom I slowly pick it up and turn it upside down. Thousands of pieces quickly fall onto the table. None of the pieces are alike. Not one is the same color, shape, or size. As I stand there staring at them, I realize what an incredible task lies before me. This challenge is one I have never faced before nor will ever face again in my entire existence, because I get only one chance at this complex problem, this puzzle. The pieces are mine from which to choose. The picture I create will be my doing and no one else's because God has given me the free will. Yet, I am confused—edge pieces, corner pieces, inner pieces, and no place to begin. I sit down in the isolated room of my mind, on the chair of my discretion, next to this vast horizon of life, and look vacantly at the possibilities.

"The room is a sanctuary, the chair is a pew, and the puzzle is my life. Unlike my mind, I am not secluded; the sanctuary is filled with hundreds of people. And I sit there, withdrawn from the mass, examining myself, praying. I have come to a point in my

life when I must make a decision that defines who I will be. Not an easy matter. I am frightened because I know I do not get a second chance once I have committed myself. It is all or nothing in the business of ministry. So I pray earnestly, seeking guidance, perimeters, and edge pieces to this problem.

"For some reason I open my eyes and stare down at the front of the room. Amid the hundreds of people present, a man looks at me and stands up. He moves to the pew where I am, sits down, and says words I will never forget. 'I don't know what it is, but God wants me to tell you He is going to use you. And I don't know if He wanted me to tell you as encouragement or simply as a confirmation, but that is His will.' Suddenly the pieces begin moving on the table. I watch in wonder as the fragments fly together. The edges suddenly are outlined, and my life begins to take shape. As this man prays for me, I stare at the table. My eyes are filled with tears because I realize that my puzzle is now being formed. It is by no means complete, but it is begun."

6
Biblical Examples of God's Call

What does the Bible have to say about all of this? How can it help us get a handle on this business about a call from God? When we open the Bible, we discover that God's call comes not only to a lot of unique people (like we saw at the end of the last chapter) but also in many unique ways.

- It can come while you are off minding your own business (Moses in Exod. 3).
- It can come knocking at your door like a Publisher's Clearing House million-dollar winner even though you are hiding out in a witness protection program (Gideon in Judg. 6).
- It can come early in life when you're not even sure what the voice of God sounds like (Samuel in 1 Sam. 3).
- It can come through the prophetic voice of a mentor who puts his arm around you and declares, "You are going to do great things for God" (Elisha in 1 Kings 19).
- It can come in an unforgettable moment of overwhelming confrontation between you and a holy God (Isaiah in Isa. 6).
- It can come and chase you down like a Whale-O-Gram while you are running away from God (Jonah in Jon. 1—3).
- It can come with just a simple tap on the shoulder

and an invitation to "[come,] follow me" (Levi in Luke 5).

- It can come like a surprise bolt of lightning that blasts you off your feet and sends you off in a radically new direction (Paul in Acts 9).

I think I'll take a break and eat dessert while these guys tell you how they heard God's call. As you listen to them, you might be surprised to find that one of their stories that sounds like your own.

An Unmistakable Call—Moses

In your advanced techno-world maybe a burning bush is no big deal. As for me, I'd never seen a burning bush before. Come to think of it, I haven't seen one since.

I was minding my own business out in the wilderness trying to be a decent shepherd. Earlier in life I thought I might be somebody important. But then I really screwed up. So, I settled for being an average guy in an average place doing average stuff. I figured that was the best life had to offer me.

Then one day God appeared and blew all my plans for mediocrity into the next galaxy. I put up a fight for a while, suggesting that He might need to find someone else. But God made it unmistakably clear that He had huge plans for me. His message was so crystal clear that I knew exactly what I was supposed to do: "You will deliver My people from the bondage of Egypt" (see Exod. 3:10).

That encounter with God was so unbelievable I had to take my shoes off. It was unforgettable. That was the day God promised to go with me and strengthen me for the challenging task that He had laid out before me. In

Sound Byte Summary from Moses

If you're going to do something great for God, you need a burning bush . . . or at least a burning heart.

the years that followed, whenever I was tempted to doubt or be afraid, I always remembered the day God gave me an unmistakable call.

An Unexpected Call—Gideon

I wish I had the confidence and the leadership style that Big Mo had. When people are choosing teams for a game of baseball, Moses is always the first to be chosen and I am always last. I'm like the little brother you have to take on your team or else Mom will shoot you.

When God came looking for me, I was hiding in the barn to keep away from the Midianites. Their army was like an F-5 tornado tearing up the Oklahoma countryside. Everybody knew that somebody ought to fight them, but I knew for sure that it wasn't going to be me.

Out of nowhere the Lord found me and rocked my world by shouting out, "The LORD is with you, mighty warrior" (Judg. 6:12). I immediately thought He was kidding, and I told Him so: "You've got the wrong number. You must want the other Gideon that lives down on Hineni Street." He said, "No, you're the one I want."

I'm embarrassed to admit it, but I made up this goofy test for God. Have you heard of my "fleece" thing? I made Him take it twice. Even tried to trick Him on the second one. Both times He "aced" it. So what would you do in a case like that? Me too. I quit arguing and told Him, "If You're crazy enough to want me, I'm all Yours." He responded, "I'm not as interested in your ability as I am in your availability."

Sound Byte Summary from Gideon

When God calls you to do something great, it's OK to be really scared. It's also OK to have doubts and questions.

Remember, God + you = a majority!

An Early Call—Samuel

I'm one of those kids who's been in church all his life. Actually I started going to church nine months before I was born. My mom and dad were great believers, loved God and loved the church. Mom tells the story of how she prayed for me to be born and how she promised to give me back to the Lord. God answered her prayer, and Mom fulfilled her promise.

Because of this great heritage, I always felt as if I was destined to serve the Lord. It's as if everything in my life prepared me to be a servant for the Lord. As long as I can remember, I have wanted to serve Him.

So it was sort of natural that very early in my life I heard God's call. In fact, it came so early I wasn't sure at first if it was really His call. I thought it might just be someone else calling me. But after talking with my pastor, he helped me realize that it really was God calling me.

I am so thankful for my mom and my dad. I'm glad they brought me up in church. I'm glad they dedicated me to the Lord. I'm glad they dreamed great dreams for me. And I'm glad for a pastor who had a tender ear that was sensitive enough to help me hear God's call with clarity and certainty.

Sound Byte Summary from Samuel

If you're going to do something great for God, it's good to get an early start!

A Human Call—Elisha

Have you heard of the kid who said, "Grandma Morris always used to grab me and pinch my cheek and say, 'Sonny Boy, one of these days you're gonna grow up and be a great preacher.'" That's my story.

In my day Elijah was "the Man." He was one of my

heroes. His prayers made the rain stop for three years. He destroyed Baal in one of the greatest WWF matches of all time. He and his foster family survived for two years on this unbelievably small amount of flour and oil. And when he was at his lowest, he was still able to hear the clear, quiet voice of God.

Do you have any idea what it's like to have someone like Elijah come up to you, put his arm around you, look you in the eye, and say to you, "God has told me that you are going to do great things for Him"? That's exactly what Elijah did to me.

To help me get started in ministry, he let me hang out with him and be his sidekick. I helped him set up chairs for our youth group services, went calling with him, learned how to pray with him, and watched him be a man of God.

To be honest with you, this whole time I wasn't sure whether or not God had called me. Everything was based on what Elijah had told me. And for a long time that was good enough for me. But there did come a day when God confirmed that it truly was His will that I fulfill the prediction that Elijah had made many years before.

Sound Byte Summary from Elisha

Sometimes God's call to greatness comes through a human voice. Don't ignore that.

A Holy Call—Isaiah

My call came one Sunday morning at church. It was as if God himself was talking directly to me. God came to me! (Does that sound weird?) He lifted me into His presence. There were angel-like beings flying all around. He showed me how holy He was, how *other* He was. This was the most intimate encounter I had ever had with God.

When I realized how great He was, I immediately realized how ungreat I was. Before, when I compared myself to my other Christian friends, I felt as if I was probably doing pretty well. But when I got a clear picture of God, I knew I was in trouble and needed serious help. I asked God to make me clean as He was. And He did. That was the day God sanctified me holy and wholly.

That was the same day I received my call. It came like a package deal. Being closer to God than I ever had been before, I could hear Him crying, saying, "Who am I going to find to take my message of salvation to the world?" I quickly responded, "Here am I. Send me." He said, "OK, let's go!"

From there, I went on to do some really great things for God. But I know none of that would have happened if I hadn't experienced that day when I got things straight with God.

Sound Byte Summary from Isaiah

Before you can do anything great for God, you need to figure out how *ungreat* you are without Him.

A Chasing Call—Jonah

I knew early on that God had called me to be a preacher. I also knew I didn't want to have any part of that plan.

I probably knew that I should do what He was telling me to do. And I knew that it would be the right thing or the best thing. I just didn't want to. I thought I knew my life better than God did. I figured I could run my life better than He could.

So I ran away from His call. I didn't just ignore it or try to pretend it didn't exist. I just flat out ran. And, of course, you know all about the fish that swallowed me up out of the ocean.

The key point of my story is that we serve a God of the second chance. Even though we fuss and run away and complain and get mad at God for not asking our advice about how to run the world, He is so patient to keep knocking at our door and asking, "Now are you ready to listen?"

In fact, all my life I've been a negative, complaining kind of person, but God has never punched my ticket and told me to take a hike. I'm so glad God never gives up on me. I'm glad He gave me a second chance to say yes to His will and His call on my life.

Sound Byte Summary from Jonah

If God has a call on your life for greatness, don't run from Him. He really does know best. Besides . . . He knows your number.

A Transforming Call—Levi

To be honest, I don't have a clue why Jesus called me to be one of His disciples. Why did He call me and not someone else? Why did He pick me out of the crowd? Why did He choose me for greatness? No clue.

I think that's how it is a lot of times. God just comes along and taps us on the shoulder and says, "Would you like to follow Me on a journey of greatness?" But then maybe He taps lots of other shoulders and it just happens that our shoulders are connected to a heart that says yes.

From my perspective Jesus' call meant three things: First, it was a call to be with Him. Before anything else, He just wanted the other disciples and me to enjoy being with Him, to build a relationship, a friendship with

Him. Second, it was a call to preparation. We needed those three years of teaching and training alongside Jesus. We learned so many lessons. From the very beginning I was ready to witness and start bringing people to Jesus. But there is no way I could have handled the long haul of ministry if it hadn't been for those years of training we had with Jesus.

Finally, Jesus' call was a call to transformation—a call not only for transformation in my own life but also for a passion to pass that life-changing message on to others. If God can take a greedy, materialistic, self-centered person like me and turn my life inside out, then I have to tell other people about what God can do in their lives.

Sound Byte Summary from Levi

If you want a long-term ministry of greatness, you gotta have three bes: be with Him, be prepared, be transformed.

An Out-of-the-Blue Call—Paul

I was your worst nightmare. I was the one who made fun of you for being a Christian. I was the one who could quote the parts of the Bible just to prove my point and make you look like a fool. I was the one who spied on you to catch you if you ever messed up. I was always causing trouble.

The bottom line is, I was the very last person anyone would have ever guessed could get a call from God. I was so mean and awful that no Christian would even try to witness to me about God. Any one of them knew I would bite off his or her head.

The only One not afraid of me was God himself. As a way of getting my attention, He unleashed this awesome laser show that literally knocked me off my feet. He didn't beat around the bush. He came straight at me and told me to get my act together.

From that moment on, my life did a complete 180. Talk about radical. At first I was radical in my hatred for Jesus, but since He got hold of my life, I have been *souled-out* and 24/7 in love with Jesus.

When I finally gave my heart to Jesus and began to follow His call for my life, we really made up for lost time. I guess it's the old thing about, "The bigger they are, the harder they fall." All I know is that when I fell for Jesus, I fell hard.

Sound Byte Summary from Paul

Sometimes when you think you've been too bad for God to use, that's when God drops His greatest plan in the middle of your heart.

7
The Ride of Your Life

How are we doing so far? We have been sitting in this booth for so long now, we're going to have to leave a big tip. Why don't we take off and go for a ride. I've got some scenery I want to show you.

As we drive north through the Central Valley of California on Highway 99, out your passenger side window is the Sierra Nevada. Out my window and not far away are the cool ocean breezes just to the west of us. Since it's a crisp spring day, the almond trees are in full blossom and the snow-covered mountain peaks are dazzling white in the warm sunlight.

We turn east on Highway 180 and head toward the mountains. We soon smell the most remarkably sweet smell ever enjoyed on planet Earth—the smell of orange blossoms in early April. Hallelujah! As we climb higher, the mountain road puts a heavy strain on our little engine. The steep inclines and sharp mountain curves demand purposeful attention. The mountains seem to rise quickly in front of us as we draw closer.

At some point we need to decide exactly where we want to go on this journey. Maybe as soon as we turned on Highway 180, we were certain of the exact peak or lake that had "our name" on it. On the other hand, perhaps all we knew was that the mountains were calling us. As we look at the map, we realize there are a number of options from which to choose. There are the majestic peaks and the crystal clear lakes that everyone talks about, but there are also ageless forests, ice-cold streams, quiet wooded paths, breathless waterfalls, hidden caves, stunning rock formations.

As we continue our journey upward, we stop at several vista points where we can look back to see the winding road behind us. We can also catch a glimpse of the climb that still awaits us. These brief moments are good opportunities to check our bearings and make sure we are headed in the right direction. Do we really want to go hiking in the mountains, or would a stroll on the beach be better?

Once we have confirmed that we were made for the mountains, we can aim more intentionally in that direction. As we arrive and get out of the car, we smell the exhilarating mountain air and realize, "This is what life is all about."

Let's Break It Down

OK, at what point in the story did you figure out the allegory? Or is it a metaphor? (I always get those two mixed up.) Just for fun, you might want to read through the story again and see how much symbolism you can figure out before I start giving you my interpretation.

"Driving north on a crisp spring day" refers to these early days on your journey of life. As a young person you have all the possibilities of life ahead of you. Opportunities are blossoming all around you. Your future is unbelievably exciting. (Remember, you're a rhino, not a cow.)

"When we turn east" symbolizes saying yes to God's definite call to full-time ministry. The truth is, you could have just as easily heard and responded to a call from

God that would have sent you westward toward the endless possibilities of secular careers over on the coast. And if that would have been His call, then you would have been 100 percent in His will to turn west and follow Him on that rewarding journey. But for whatever reason, you have heard God's voice echoing from the mountains calling you to a life in ministry that will be challenging and fulfilling.

"Highway 180" plays an extremely important role in this analogy. Highway 180 is the path of preparation for ministry that you need to give special attention to. Just because you can see the mountain peaks from Highway 99 does not mean that you can hear God's call one day and jump into full-time ministry the next. A call to ministry is a call to preparation. That is so critical, you need to hear it again. A call to ministry is a call to preparation.

My friend Jeremy is a senior in high school. Here's how he described his struggle with Highway 180. "The biggest difficulty that I've experienced is patience. On more than one occasion I have been told that a call to ministry is a call to prepare. I have an urgency about getting out and being in the ministry now. I perceive college almost like time wasted. My pastor has told me that I should plan for college and perhaps even seminary. I am taking his advice because it will benefit me more in the long run. Plus not too many churches are willing to take an unschooled, 19-year-old kid on their staffs. Probably a wise decision."

Great ministry requires great preparation. One old preacher said, "If I had 10 years to do ministry, I'd spend 4 of them in preparation." It's amazing to realize that Jesus spent 30 years in preparation compared to only 3 in actual ministry.

The church needs you to be a sharp, well-educated minister. The congregations you serve in the future will be looking to you every Sunday for spiritual direction.

God needs you to be intellectually prepared to meet the challenges of your society and culture. You need to have a clear understanding of:

The Bible	The Church
Christian theology	Church history
Philosophy	Worship
Missions	Evangelism
Spiritual formation	Christian holiness
Preaching skills	Counseling skills
Relational skills	Leadership skills

Do you think you're going to find all of that in a McDonald's Happy Meal? I doubt it.

In addition to all this ministerial preparation, you also need a solid education in the general areas of science, history, English composition, literature, fine arts, business, and so on, in order to be well-balanced. As you "climb higher in elevation" (education), you will feel the

> A call to ministry
> is
> a call to preparation

brain strain that comes from trying to carve new wrinkles into your gray matter. There will be times when you feel like a saturated sponge and be disgusted to find that you're only a junior with another two years of college ahead of you and then seminary.

But before you panic and crash on these sharp mountain curves, let me assure you that you don't have to get straight A's all the time. You just want to do your best. As Paul said, you want to be purposeful in "[pressing] on toward the goal to win the prize for which God has called me heavenward in Christ Jesus" (Phil. 3:14).

I will never forget the day in the 11th grade when Mrs. Strickland challenged me to give my best rhino effort in my schoolwork. We were in English Composition. I was complaining that my paper was as good as the guys around me, and therefore I should have received the same grade. Mrs. Strickland told me she wanted to see me out in the hallway. I thought I was in big trouble. She put her hand on my shoulder and spoke unforgettable words to my tender heart. She said, "Doug, I know who you are and what you plan to be in life. The rest of these kids are just going to be doctors and lawyers and businesspeople. But you are going to be a pastor. That is the most important job in all the world. I'm sorry if it's not fair sometimes, but I expect more out of you than I do everyone else."

Wow! From that moment on she was my favorite teacher. I learned more from her than from anyone else. Throughout my college and seminary years I wrote all my papers exactly the way Mrs. Strickland taught me.

I wish I could be your Mrs. Strickland. (Or maybe Mr. Strickland.) Wherever you are on Highway 180, I want to challenge you to begin now to prepare yourself with a great education. If you are still in your junior high or senior high years, make the most of these early years of school. Develop good study habits and cultivate a joy of learning that will carry you through life.

You will also want to make plans to attend a Christian college or university where you can continue your education. It is possible that upon graduation from college you will feel ready and prepared to take a position of ministry in a local church. However, you might find that it would be worthwhile to pursue graduate studies toward a master's degree.

As you can tell from this lengthy discussion of Highway 180, the educational preparation for ministry is extremely important. The sooner you discover the discipline of being a lifelong learner, the better off you will be.

"The sweet aroma of orange blossoms . . ." Somewhere along this Highway 180 you will probably find a spouse who will be the sweet aroma of your life. Your spouse will become your best friend, your prayer partner, your lover, your fellow dreamer, and the joy of your life. So be careful in your dating practices not to fall in love with a cow. Nuff said.

"The peaks, lakes, streams, forests, and so on" are designed to portray the many options available in the field of ministry. As mentioned in the story, your call to ministry may come with a distinct call to a specific area, such as missions or youth ministry. On the other hand, you might be certain about God's call to ministry but not have a clue as to the exact ministry He has for you.

The important thing for now is to be aware of the various roles in which a minister might serve. You could be a:

Pastor	Missionary
Youth pastor	Children's pastor
Minister of music	Deacon
Administrative pastor	Church planter
Chaplain	Evangelist
Educator	Urban specialist

In the years ahead, as the church looks for ways to meet the needs of our society, there will undoubtedly be new categories added on a regular basis.

Another issue for you to consider is the possibility that over time your understanding of your call might change. From my early years of junior high school, I had a clear call to be a missionary. But when I was in seminary, God put me through a painful six-month process where that call was changed to youth ministry. Then after 1 year of youth ministry, God closed that door and sent me into pastoral ministry. After 22 years of pastoring, God has now moved me into the teaching ministry. Who knows what else He has planned for me?

Be careful not to lock God's call into one specific kind of ministry role. As you learn more about your own gifts and abilities, give God the freedom to direct you to the area where He knows you would fit best.

"Vista points" are the wide places along the journey where you catch your breath and refocus yourself. Some of you may feel right now that God has given you a definite call to full-time ministry. But there may come a time when you're not sure about things. If that happens, you will want to find a place to pull off the road and check your bearings.

My friend Roger Hahn teaches at Nazarene Theological Seminary. Listen to how he explains this gut-check process: "Should you begin to question your call, you will not be the first person to do so. You should prayerfully consider your sense of calling and ways in which the church has enthusiastically or hesitatingly affirmed your call. You will want to talk about your questions with trusted, mature Christian friends, including your pastor and/or professors.

"Do not be hasty in deciding that you misinterpreted a call or are no longer called. If, after careful prayer and consideration, you decide that you misinterpreted a call or are no longer called, do not take that as a sign of spiritual failure. God will make use of all your learning and development in His time.

"Do not let well-intentioned friends or acquaintances make you feel guilty for your change in understanding God's will for your life. It is better to deal with a mistaken call or a new direction in your life when you know that it has happened rather than to continue preparing out of a false sense of duty or the desire to please someone else."

It is probably normal to go through periods of questioning your call. And it's good to struggle with your call so you are forced to make crystal clear that God has called you to the ministry. One of my old professors told me one time, "If you can do anything other than be a preacher and still get to heaven, you better do it because there will be lots of days that you wish you could go do something else."

If God settles your doubts and answers all your questions, then you can feel confident in moving on up the mountain.

"This is what life is all about." My prayer for you is that if you have truly sensed a call from God to full-time ministry, you will be faithful to the long process of preparation. Then, I trust, once you are out there on your own (with God's help and your spouse's encouragement), you will be able to say with confidence, "This is what life is all about. This is my destiny. This is what God designed me for. This is my calling. This is my life."

Enjoy the Journey!

Well, the allegorical journey was a lot quicker than the explanatory journey. I hope this was helpful. I wanted to give you a preview of what to expect in the years ahead. Hopefully this scenic tour answered some of your questions and encouraged you to stay focused on your dreams of doing great things for God.

8
So, What Do I Do Now?

Now that you're back home after the scenic tour of the mountain, what are you supposed to be doing? If you know that God has called you into the ministry, and if that ministry is still some years away, what do you do in the meantime?

Once you go away to college and actually start your classes in theology and ministry, you will quickly pick up speed on your climb up the mountain. But you may have a couple years remaining in high school. Is there anything you can do right now to strengthen your call?

I posed that question to some of my college friends who are just a few years ahead of you on the ministerial journey. I'll let them tell you what they did to help strengthen their call when they were in high school. Their suggestions centered around three main issues.

1. Get involved now.
2. Find a spiritual mentor or mentors.
3. Keep listening and stay obedient.

1. Get Involved Now

"Get involved. Participate in your local and district events. Be a leader. I have taught in VBS and also taught a children's Sunday School class. I have gone on two mission trips to Mexico and participated in urban plunge projects." —Stephanie

"I taught a VBS class and currently teach the pre-

teen Sunday School class. Anything you can do around the church, especially where you get to teach, is a wonderful experience. I even got to lead our Sunday evening devotional a couple of times. It's much easier to get up in front of people you know than people you don't know. And they will always give you free advice for 'next time' after you're done." —Andrew

"Since God gave me a clear call to the ministry, I have worked harder to be involved as a leader in my youth group and in my church." —Paige

"I was involved with Youth for Christ at my high school. My freshman year there were only 2 people at the See You at the Pole celebration. The next year we had 10, the next we had 20, and my senior year we had 50 people come. I was so excited I started to cry." —Alma

"I led a Bible study in my home. It was usually pretty small, only five or six other teens in attendance, but it was an awesome experience." —Ben

"Since we can't just go jump on an airplane and fly off somewhere to start 'really ministering,' we need to just jump in and start right where we are." —Chad

"A call to ministry for later in life is useless if it is not accompanied with action right now. I have always tried to be a good witness to my non-Christian friends at school. Living and sharing my faith in that non-Christian environment has been my biggest challenge and weakness. But I am convinced that being a consistent Christian throughout four years of high school has made an impact on my friends, since consistency and being real are what most people today are looking for. Learning to step outside my

comfort zone and become more intentional about sharing my faith has been a great way to nurture my call."
—Brad

The message from these ministerial students should come through loud and clear. If you plan to be involved in ministry as your calling in life, you need to begin that life of ministry right now. Find ways to get involved in the life of your church. Volunteer to be a helper in Sunday School, VBS, or children's church. Commit yourself to being a leader within your teen group. Help your teen friends plug in and be supportive of your youth group. Help your friends learn to worship and pay attention to your pastor. (Someday that might be you up there.) Ask God to help you find ways to be a faithful witness for Christ even if it means sometimes having to take a stand all by yourself. Don't wait for an airplane to take you somewhere else to do something great for God; practice doing great stuff right where God has placed you.

2. Find a Spiritual Mentor or Mentors

"The most important thing for me was to find a spiritual mentor. When life turns you upside down and everything gets mixed up in your head, you need someone to lean on, someone who can give you good wisdom and guidance. My youth pastor allowed me to come alongside of him and be his partner in ministry. He taught me about leading worship, being sensitive to people's needs, and other ministry lessons. He was always supportive and willing to take time to let me vent my questions and fear. Most of all, it's great to know you have someone praying for you as you try to understand your call." **—Nathan**

"I'm the kind of person who likes to ask lots of questions, so I have always needed several significant people close to me with whom I could talk. As I

have wrestled with my call, it has been helpful to have had pastors, parents, and close friends with exceptional wisdom to help me sort things out. One pastor especially took the time to listen to all my questions and let me know it was OK to ask them. Sometimes I think he could see the pastor in me more than I could." —Chris

"Both my pastor and my youth pastor have gone out of their way to help me follow my call. They've told me how it was for them as they worked through their own calls. They've been available for me to ask questions and helped me think through my options. They showed me how they prepared sermons, and then they gave me opportunity to do the same and let me preach at our church on several occasions." —Jeremy

"My youth pastor let me spend a lot of time with him. We became best of friends. We had a Bible study together, and that is where I learned to become 100 percent real with God. He helped me see behind the scenes of ministry and talked with me about the appropriate role of a pastor. He taught me that ministry was a marathon and not a 100-yard dash." —Zach

"During my junior high years my youth pastor and his wife were wonderful. They provided me with lots of opportunities for ministry. Even though I was young, they recognized that I was ready to learn. They helped me develop many of my talents in areas such as leadership and organization." —Mary

I hope you can see how important it is to have a mentor or mentors in your life. You need to find someone you can talk to about your feelings, someone who can encourage you, someone who can offer guidance and wisdom. As you can tell from my friends, it is really great if your pastor or youth pastor can serve as your mentor. For some of you, it may be your mom or dad who becomes your spiritual partner on this journey.

If you are having trouble finding a mentor, you might want to ask your pastor or some other close friend to read this chapter and then ask him or her to consider being your mentor. Be sure to make this a matter of prayer, and ask God to guide you to the right person. If you keep striking out, remember to be a rhino and be persistent until you find one.

3. Keep Listening and Stay Obedient

"I can't remember any one specific thing that people have said to me about my call. It seems as if all of their comments have melted together into one basic piece of advice: 'Keep your heart tender and stay obedient to His leading.'" —Brad

"Say yes to God, and don't let your own plans get in the way." —Kelli

"You need to be careful to hear God's voice clearly. Make sure you are called. You're going to be doing this for the rest of your life, so you need to make sure that your call is actually a call from God and not just your own neat idea." —Stephanie

"Ever since the night I finally prayed through on my call, I have tried to stay true to that call. More than that, I have tried to stay open to God's will. Anything He wants from me is His. I just keep listening for His voice. As for now, I am confident that He wants me to pursue the mission field. But if this would ever change, I wouldn't hesitate to follow Him in a different direction. I have had times when I have doubted my calling, but God has been faithful. He has never left me. He continually reaffirms His call

on my life. So I'm trusting Him and following Him the best that I can." —Rodger

The key thought here is for you to stay tuned in to God's voice and keep listening for details. As you grow in your spiritual life and mature in your understanding of the call, God will be able to show you more clearly what He has in store for you. Listen for His direction in sermons, guest speakers, and missionaries. Learn to enjoy His refreshing presence in your worship and your personal prayer life. Keep your heart tender to His whispers; don't make Him yell at you to get your attention.

Prayer Is like Duct Tape

A Final Word from Josh

"I can wrap up my journey so far with three things: have faith, trust God, and pray. Following God's call has forced me to step out on so much faith. I am in this thing way over my head. So, I have to trust God in new ways, which has caused me to make sure what I'm doing is really His will and not mine. And then prayer. It's like duct tape: it will fix anything. It's the universal solution to all problems." —Josh

Conclusion
You Need a Pilot Light

What an unbelievable privilege you have given me to be a part of your life through the pages of this book. I have tried to use our time together to communicate to you some of the passionate fires that burn inside my heart. But I've saved the best for last. These final pages hold the pilot light that makes all the fires possible. If you miss this stuff, all that has gone before will become nothing.

Before we get started, I need to make sure everyone knows what a pilot light is. Many of you have grown up in an all-electric home and perhaps have never seen a pilot light. If you lift the top of a gas-powered stove, you will find a tiny flame that burns continually. When you turn the knob on the stove, you release the gas and this tiny flame, called the pilot light, ignites the fire for the burners on the stove. (Sorry, but that's the extent of my science/mechanical knowledge.) The point is, if you don't have the pilot light, you will never have the fire.

The Pilot Light

Throughout these pages I have done my best to challenge you to let your life burn bright for God. I've tried to communicate to you how much God hates mediocrity and how He has designed your life for greatness. I've tried to help you see how much God wants you to be a great person, how much He wants you to discover that He has great plans for your life. I've tried to make it unmistakably clear that no matter whether you are called to the ministry or to some other lifework, you need to do something great for God with your life. I've tried to encourage you to be a rhino for Jesus. Oh, how I want your life to be ablaze for God.

But I need to make sure you know how all these fires of greatness come into being. **You and I do not create these fires on our own. The only reason we have great fires in our lives is because we have Jesus, the Pilot Light, in our hearts. He is the One who ignites all the other fires. Without the Pilot Light, all we are is a bunch of smelly gas.** (This is the most important part of the whole book. Would you go back and read it again to make sure you don't miss it. And read it really slow.)

I want to do something great with my life. And I really want you to do great stuff with your life. But when great things happen in our lives, we need to remember who's the Pilot Light and who's the gas. We don't do great stuff and then take the credit for it. We don't do great stuff and think it originated from within us. We don't do great stuff and then get full of pride because of how we are so great.

Now, let's be honest. If we decide to pursue God's call for our lives and we surrender our will to His plan, then great things are going to happen. And when God accomplishes those great things in and through our lives, it is very easy to hear the applause and the cheers of others and think it's because of who we are.

Who Do the Cheers Belong To?

When each of the churches I pastored experienced healthy growth, I received a lot of church growth awards. Since I am fairly smart and like to study hard, I have several graduate degrees hanging on my wall. Since I have a crazy, rhino personality, there's a bunch of college kids who think I'm an OK prof.

But let me tell you what I know down in the core of my being: all of that great stuff would be nothing more than smelly gas if it were not for Jesus being the Pilot Light who lights my fire.

As a result, I am *always* aware that I am *always* a servant of the King. Although I strive for greatness, I am aware that if that greatness happens, it is because of Jesus. Because of all He gives to me, I live my life as a gift of thanks to my Heavenly Father. Because I have chosen to make Jesus the Lord and Master of my life, I know the following things to be true:

- It is in Him that I "live and move and have [my] being" (Acts 17:28).
- It is through His strength that "I can do all things" (Phil. 4:13, NKJV).
- I know that apart from Him I can't do anything great (John 15:5).
- I am painfully aware that if there is any "hope of glory" in me, it comes from Christ (Col. 1:27).
- In a crazy way, it is good to know that after I have done anything that someone calls great, my response is to say, "I am nothing more than a lowly servant who was simply doing my job" (Luke 17:10).
- I know how fortunate I am to have the treasure of Christ in my very "earthen vessel" (2 Cor. 4:7, NKJV).
- It is my hope that when people see my good works, all the glory would go to my Father (Matt. 5:16).

Fan the Flame

Do something great for God with your life. If He designs you and calls you to be a truck driver, be a great one. If He designs you and calls you to be a pastor, be a great one. And remember to always give Him all the glory.

Free

Leader's Guide Available at www.bhillkc.com

Visit our web site to download the *Call Waiting* leader's guide for free. The leader's guide consists of four sessions of discussion questions, activities, and scripture readings designed to help students reflect on what they've read and get the most out of the material. The leader's guide is completely free, and you can make copies of the discussion questions for use in your study.

To download the leader's guide, go to **www.bhillkc.com**. Type *Call Waiting* into the search engine at the bottom of the page. After the search engine takes you to the next page, click the link on the book's title. Scroll to the bottom of that page and under the section that reads Media Mix (Samples). There will be four links that will take you to the pages where you can download for free the four sessions of the leader's guide.

You will need Adobe Acrobat Reader to download the *Call Waiting* leader's guide. This software is free and available for download at **www.adobe.com**.